Do you like to watch the
rain pour down from the
sky, soaking trees and plants
and streets and sidewalks?

Then, right after it
rains, do you ever put
on your boots and jump
in the puddles?

When the sun comes out,
everything dries up,

and the puddles disappear.
Where do they go?

Puddles dry up because of the sun. Heat from the sun warms the smallest parts of each drop of water.

Warm air rises, and the tiny bits of water rise, too. They become part of the air. This is called evaporation.

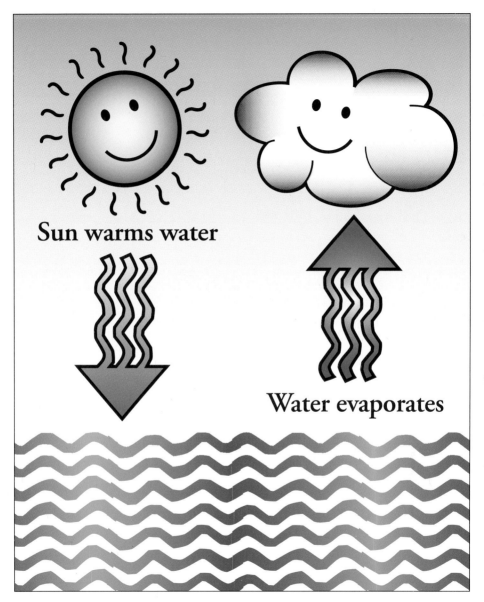

Sun warms water

Water evaporates

Water that has evaporated
is called water vapor.

Water vapor is invisible —
you can't see it.

If you can't see it, how
do you know it's there?
Here's one way to prove it.
Set a glass of ice water in
the sun.

Soon, water will start to drip down the outside of the glass. It didn't leak out of the glass; it's water that was in the air.

When water vapor is cooled, it turns back into water. This is called condensation.

Water vapor rises high into the sky.

The air is cooler up there, so the water vapor condenses. Tiny water droplets join with other droplets, and soon there are so many droplets in one place that you can see them.

That's what clouds are.

There are different kinds
of clouds. Some are big
and puffy and white.

Some are so full of water that they turn gray. Then, heavy drops of water fall to the ground as rain.

If it is cold enough outside,
it snows instead.

Rainwater doesn't always evaporate right away. A lot of it trickles into streams and rivers.

The streams and rivers
flow into lakes and oceans.
The sun heats them up
like giant puddles.

Water on the surface
evaporates, rises into
the sky, collects as clouds,
and falls as rain again.

This pattern is called
the water cycle.

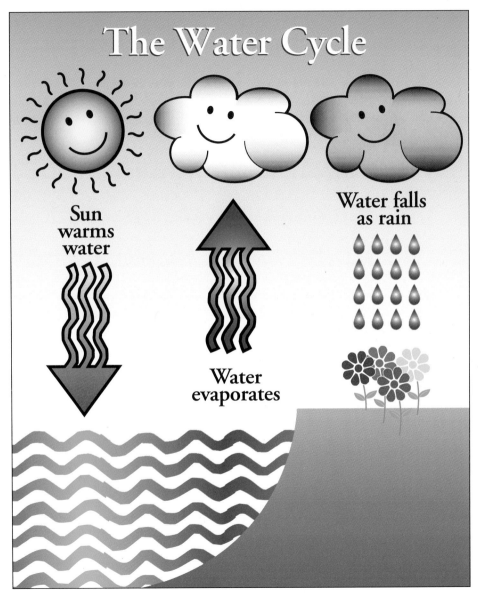

The water cycle never stops.
All the water we have on
Earth is all we ever had.
From prehistoric times until
now, the same water is used
over and over and over again.

That's one good reason
to take care of it.

The water you use today

may someday fall in a
mountain snowstorm,

crash over a cliff in a waterfall,

spout from a whale
in an ocean,

Words You Know

water cycle

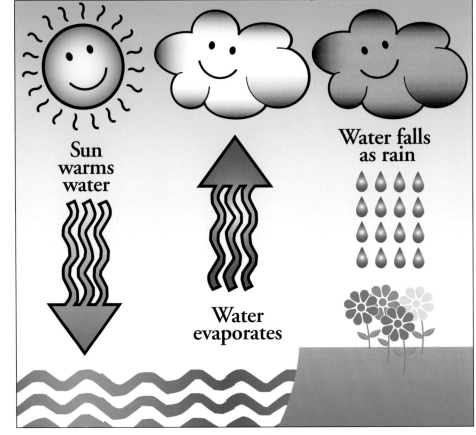

Sun
warms
water

Water
evaporates

Water falls
as rain

sun   evaporation

rain

puddle

waterfall

clouds

condensation

whales   ocean

Index

About the Author

Fay Robinson is an early childhood specialist who lives and works in the Chicago area. She received a bachelor's degree in Child Study from Tufts University and a master's degree in Education from Northwestern University. She has taught preschool and elementary children and is the author of several picture books.

Photo Credits

Photri – ©Michael Habicht, 23

PhotoEdit – ©Robert Brenner, 3, 5, 31 (top left); ©David Young-Wolff, 6, 7, 11, 12, 31 (bottom left); ©Paul S. Conklin, 22

SuperStock International, Inc. – ©Edmond E. Van Hoorick, 16; ©Robert Llewellyn, 18, 29, 31 (top right); ©P. & R. Manley, 26, 31 (center left)

Tony Stone Images – ©Trevor Mein, 17; ©Kevin Schafer, 27, 31 (bottom right)

Valan – ©Wayne Shiels, Cover; ©Don McPhee, 15, 31 (center right); ©Bob Gurr, 19; ©John Eastcott/Yva Momatiuk, 24; ©J.R. Page, 25

Electronic Illustration: Feldman & Associates, Inc. – ©Anna Keller/Bill Ewing, 9, 21, 30

COVER: Child exploring puddle